NATIONAL GEOGRAPHIC

T0040046

I Like Being Outdoors

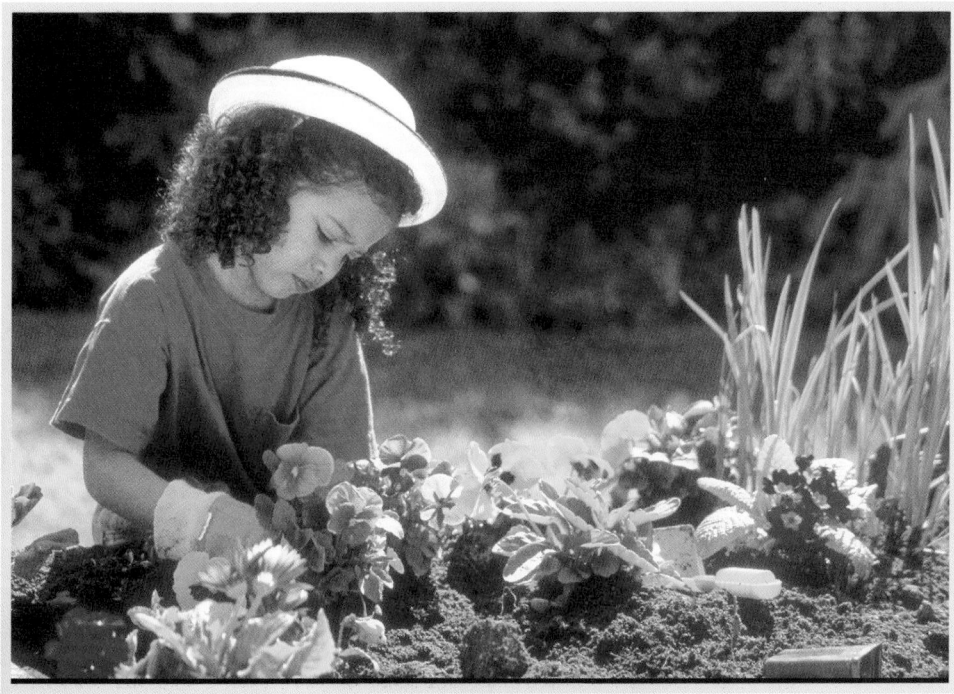

Wil Spencer

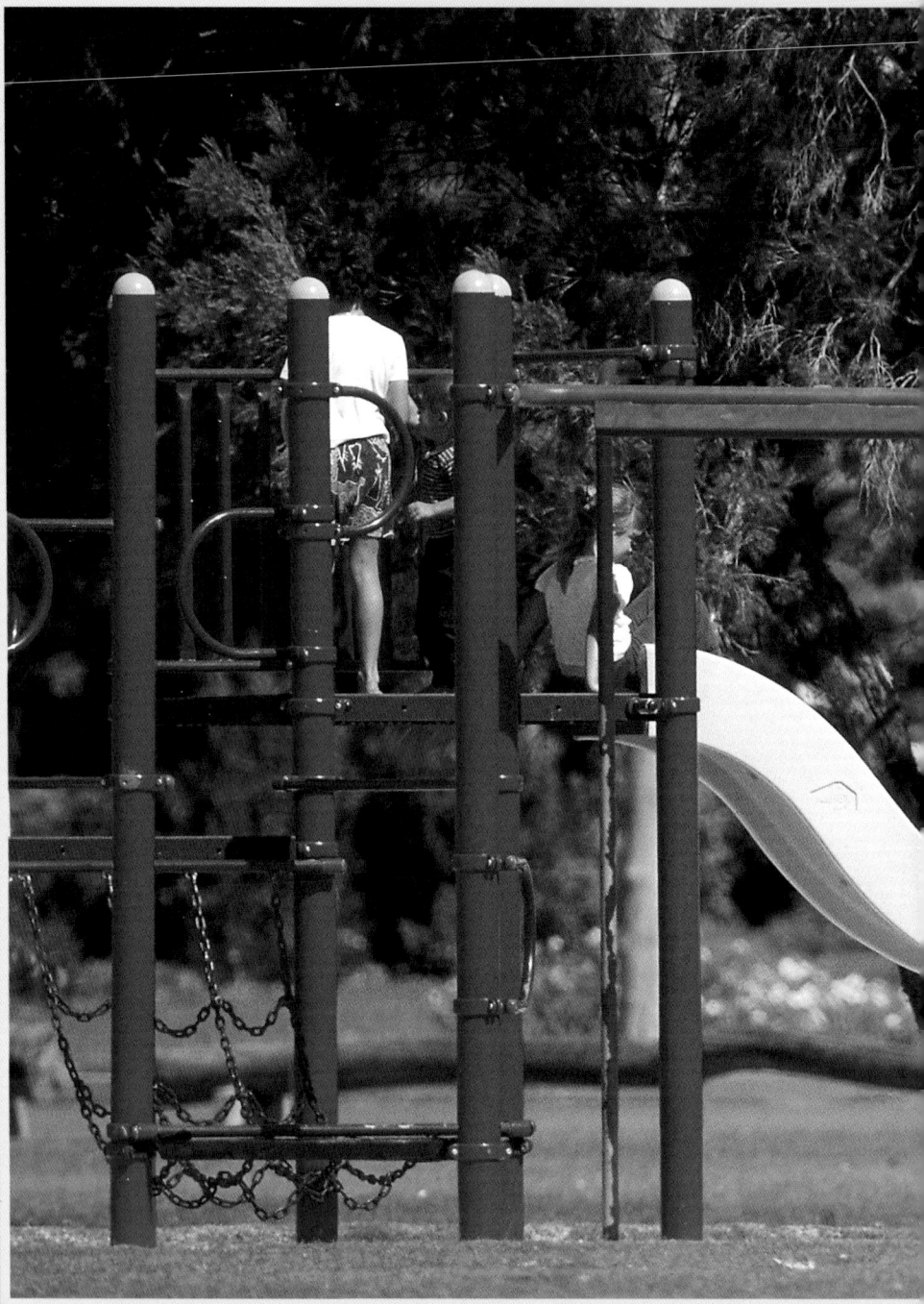

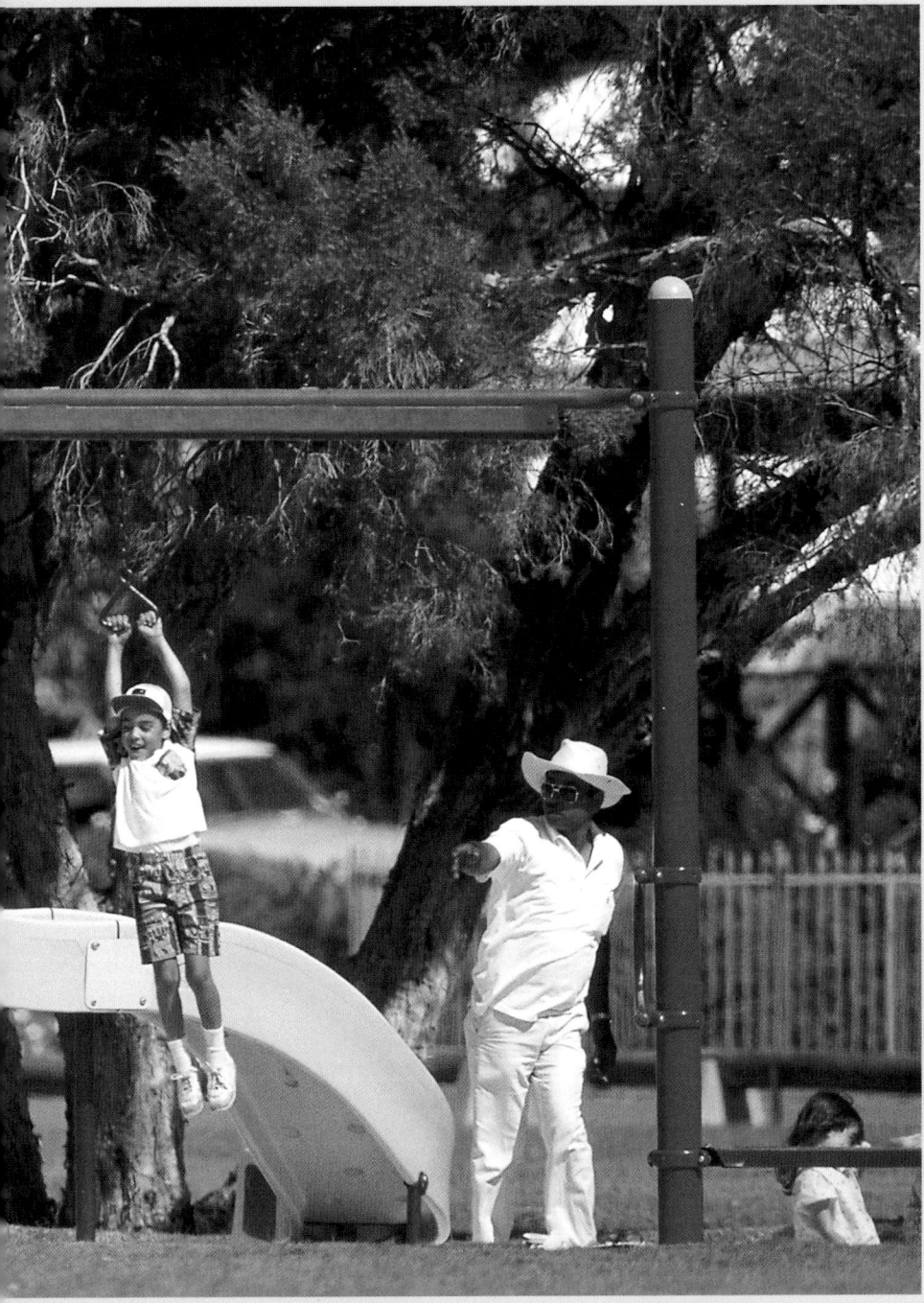

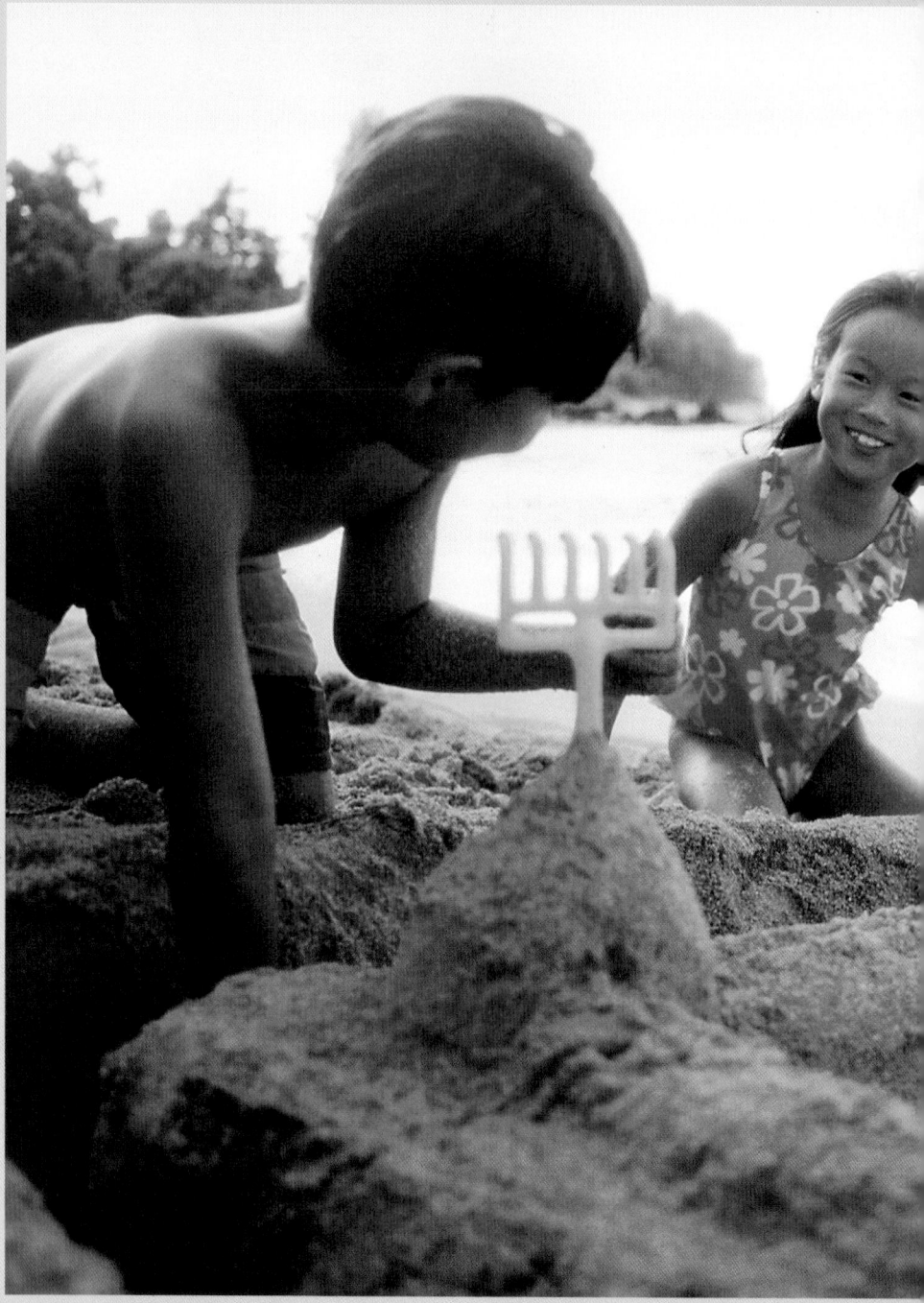

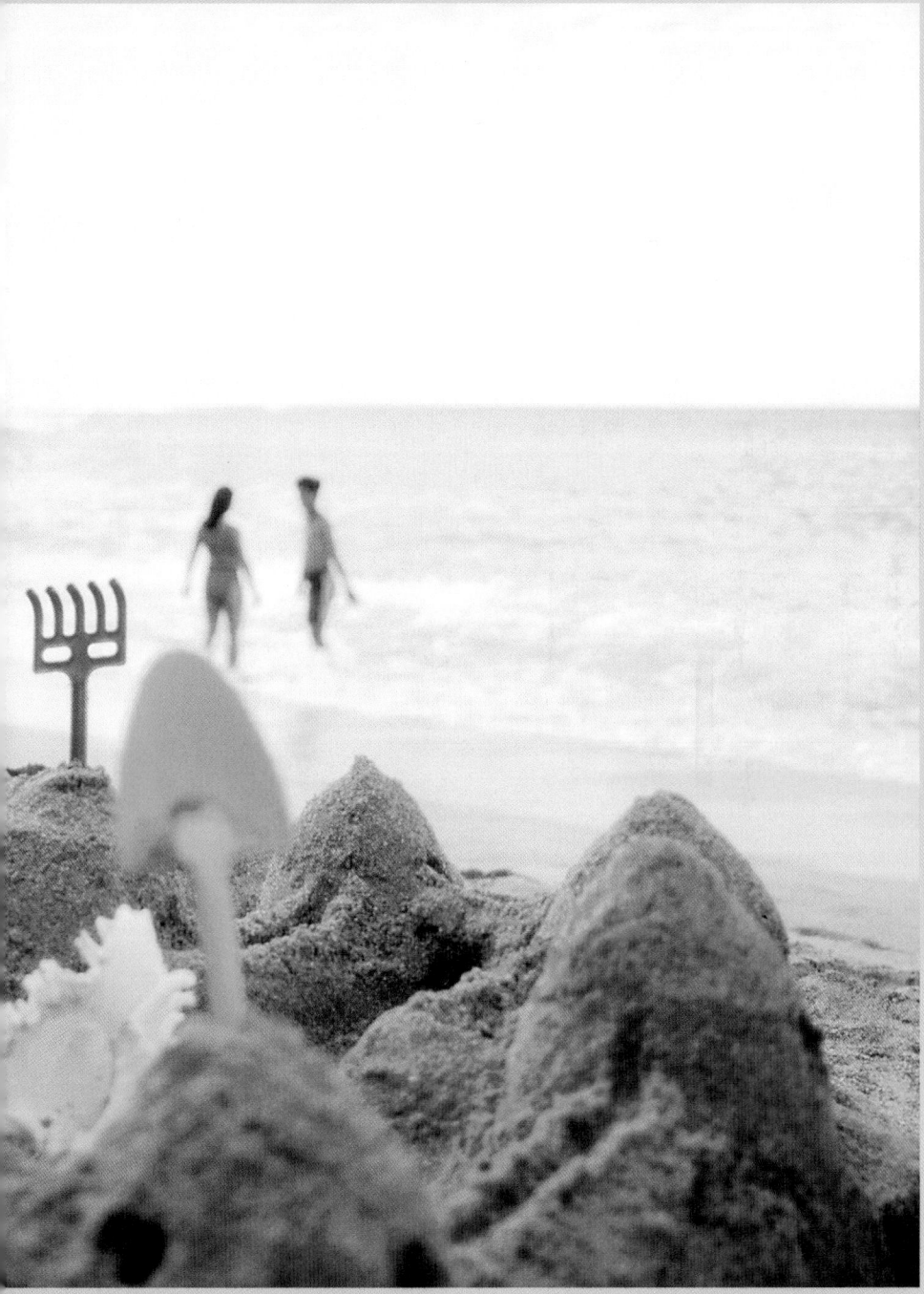

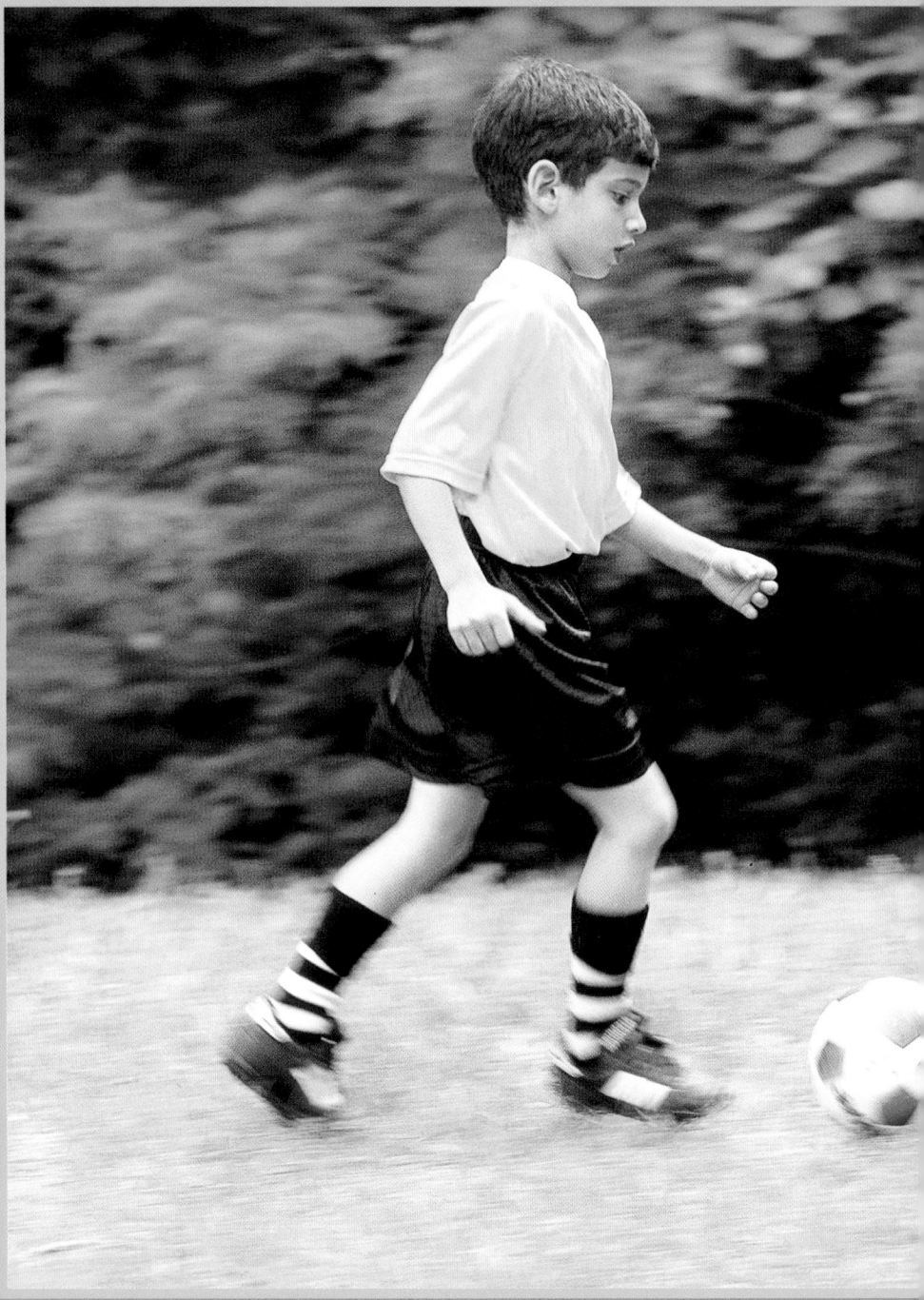

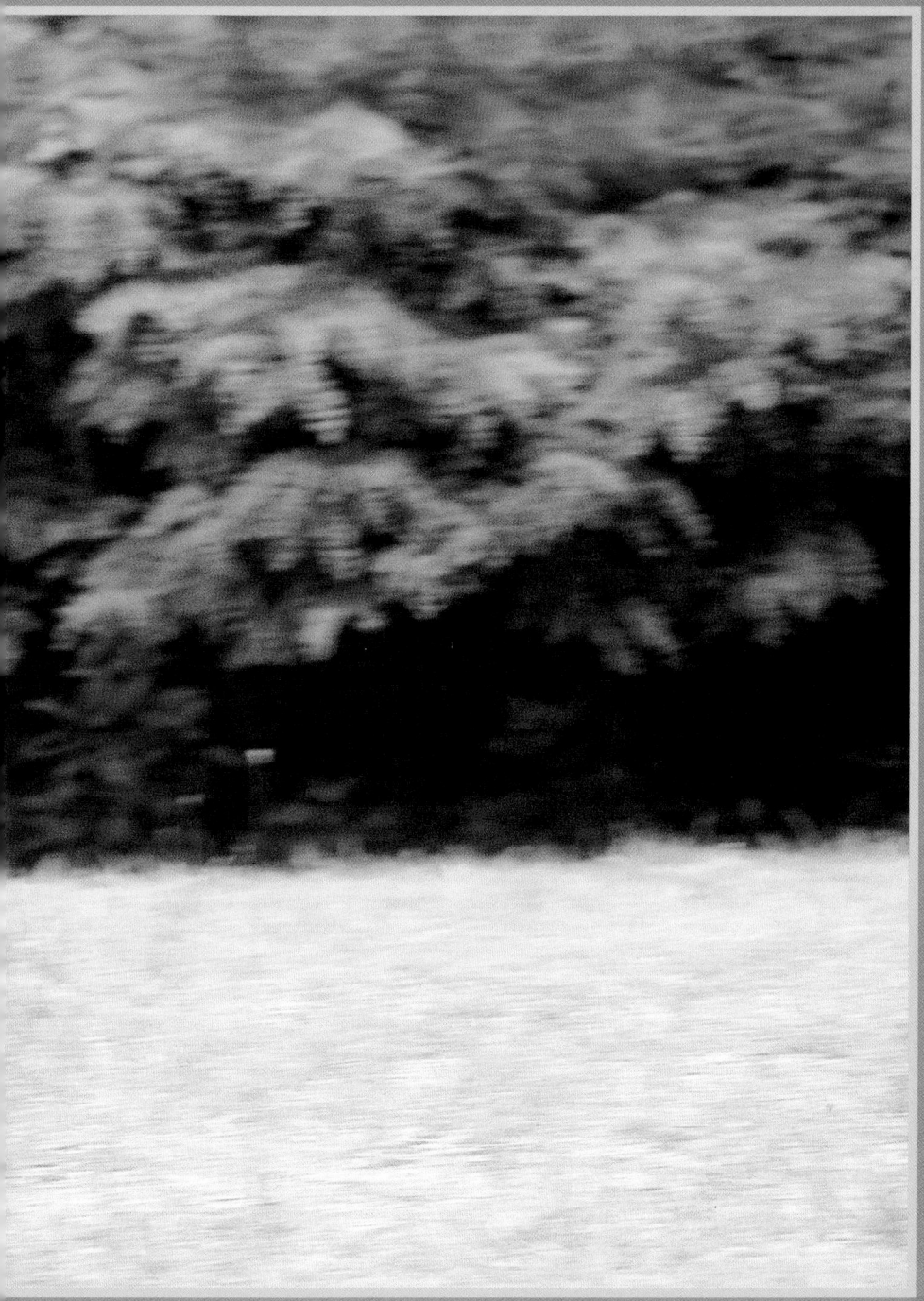

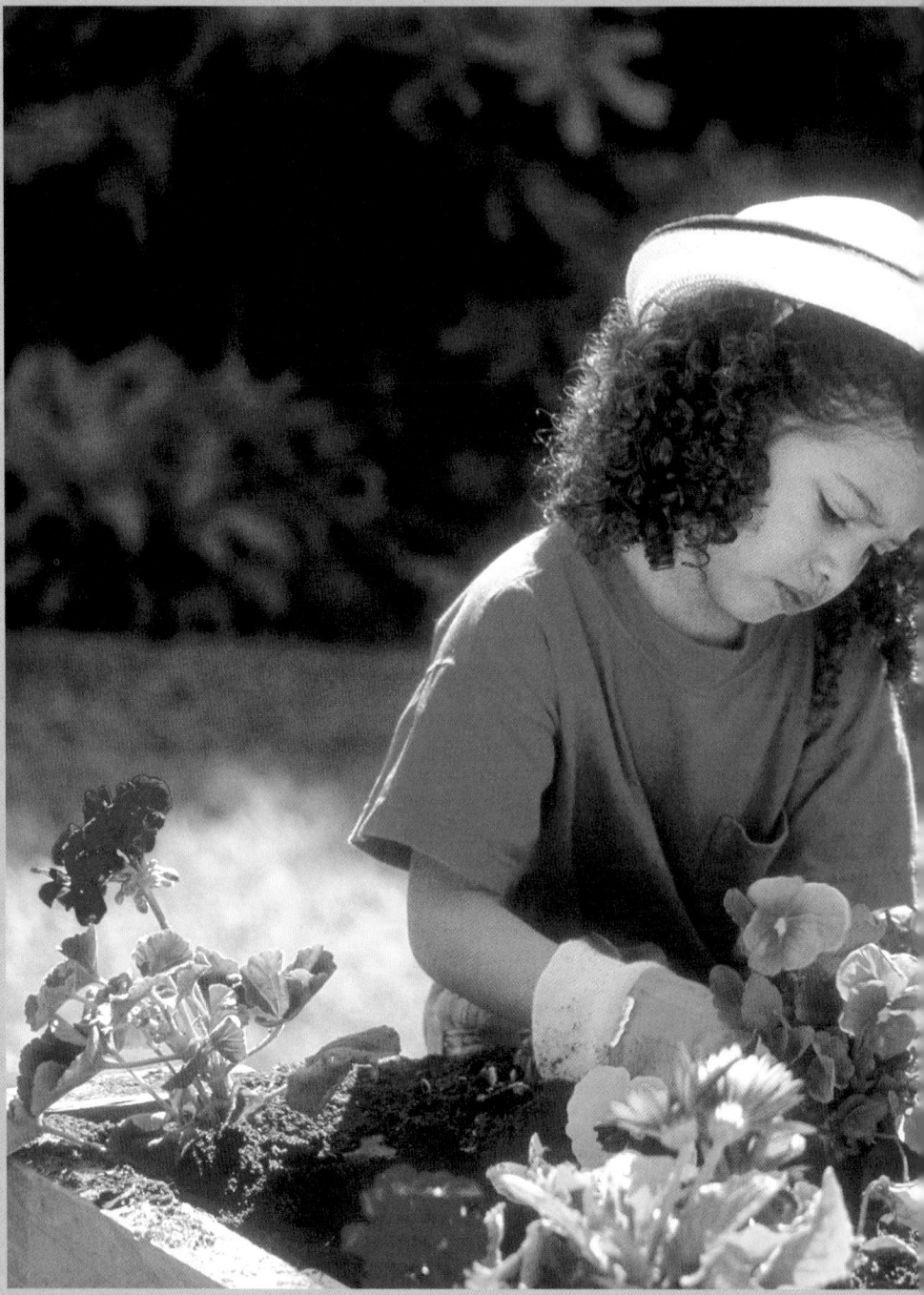

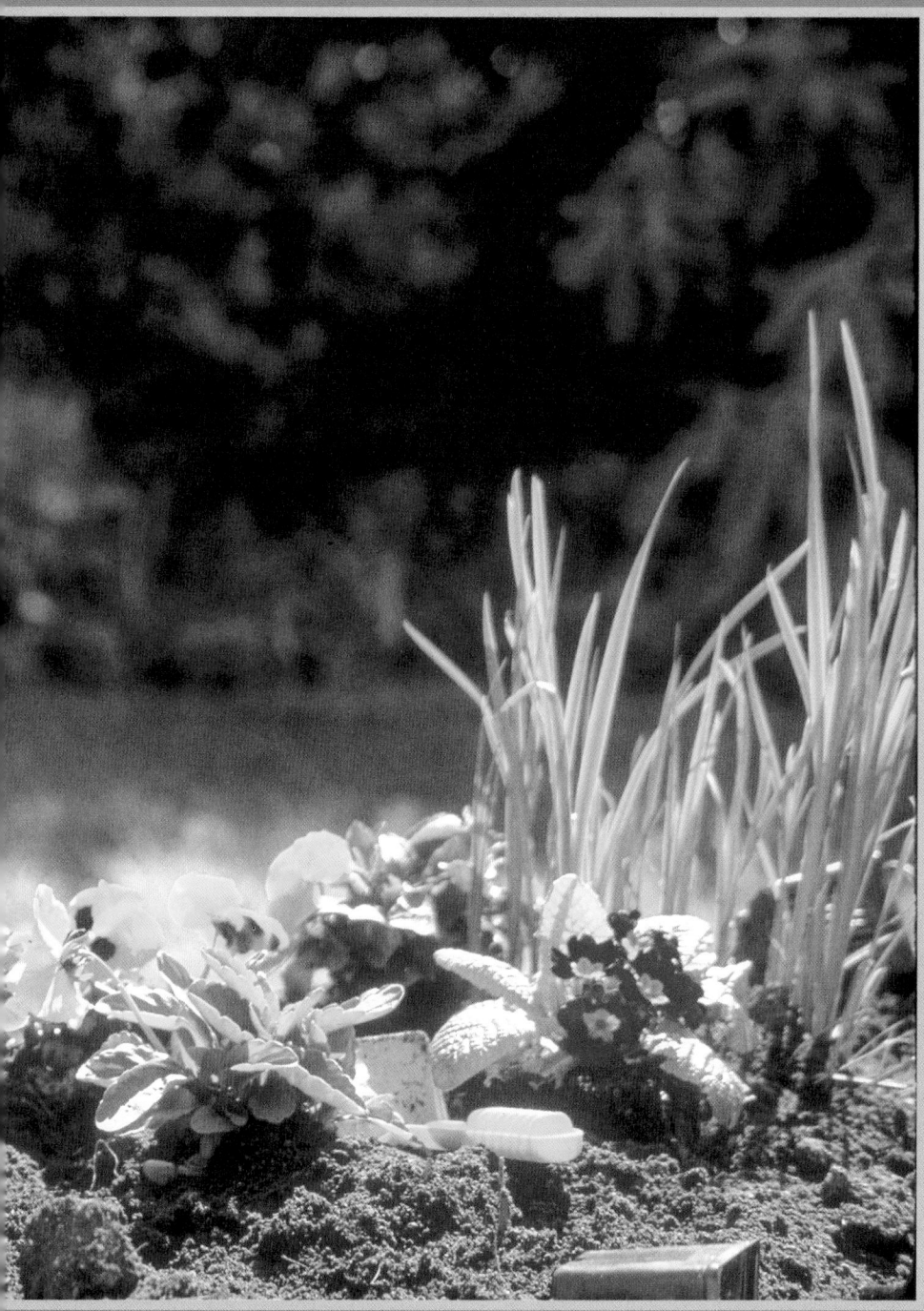

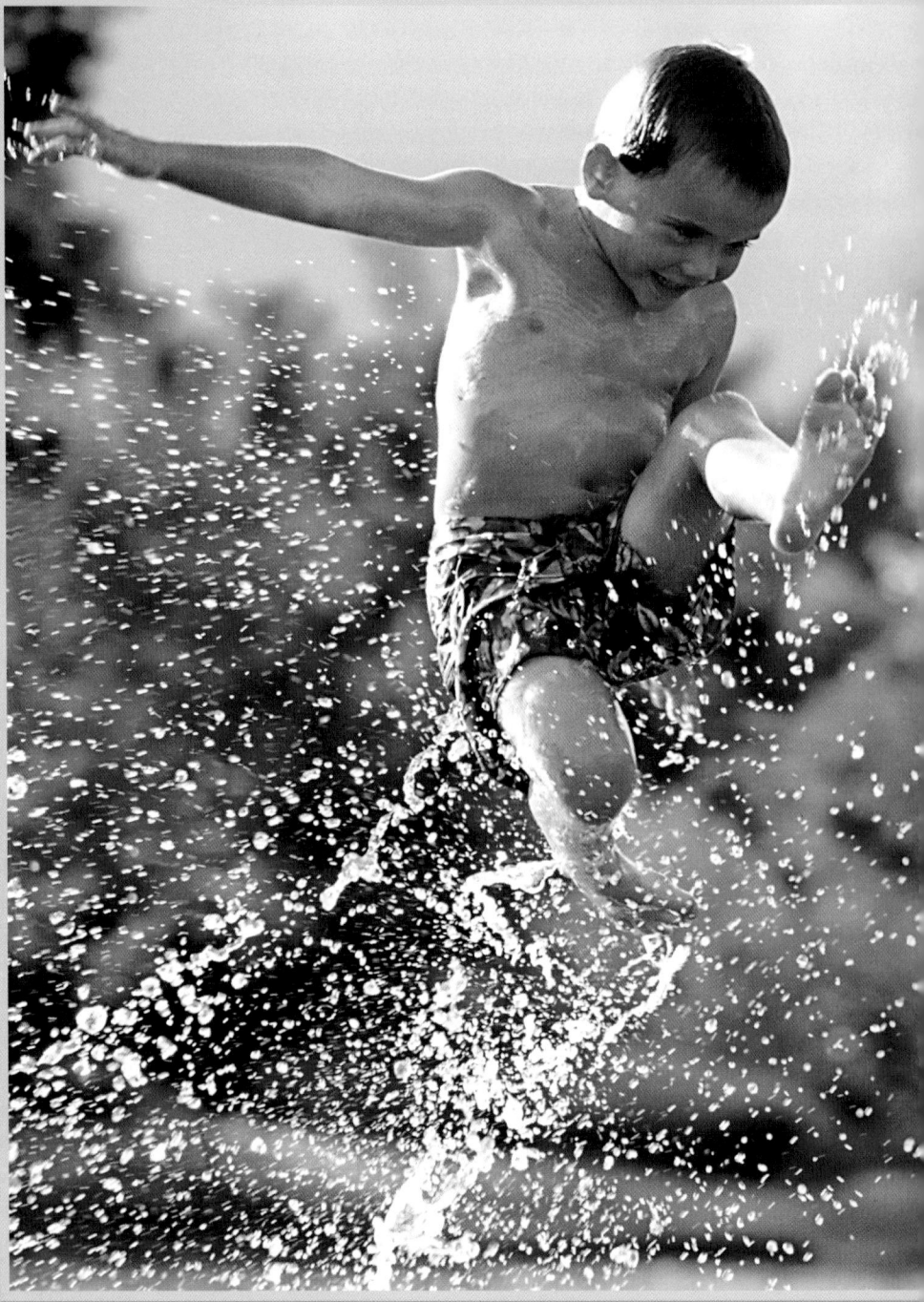

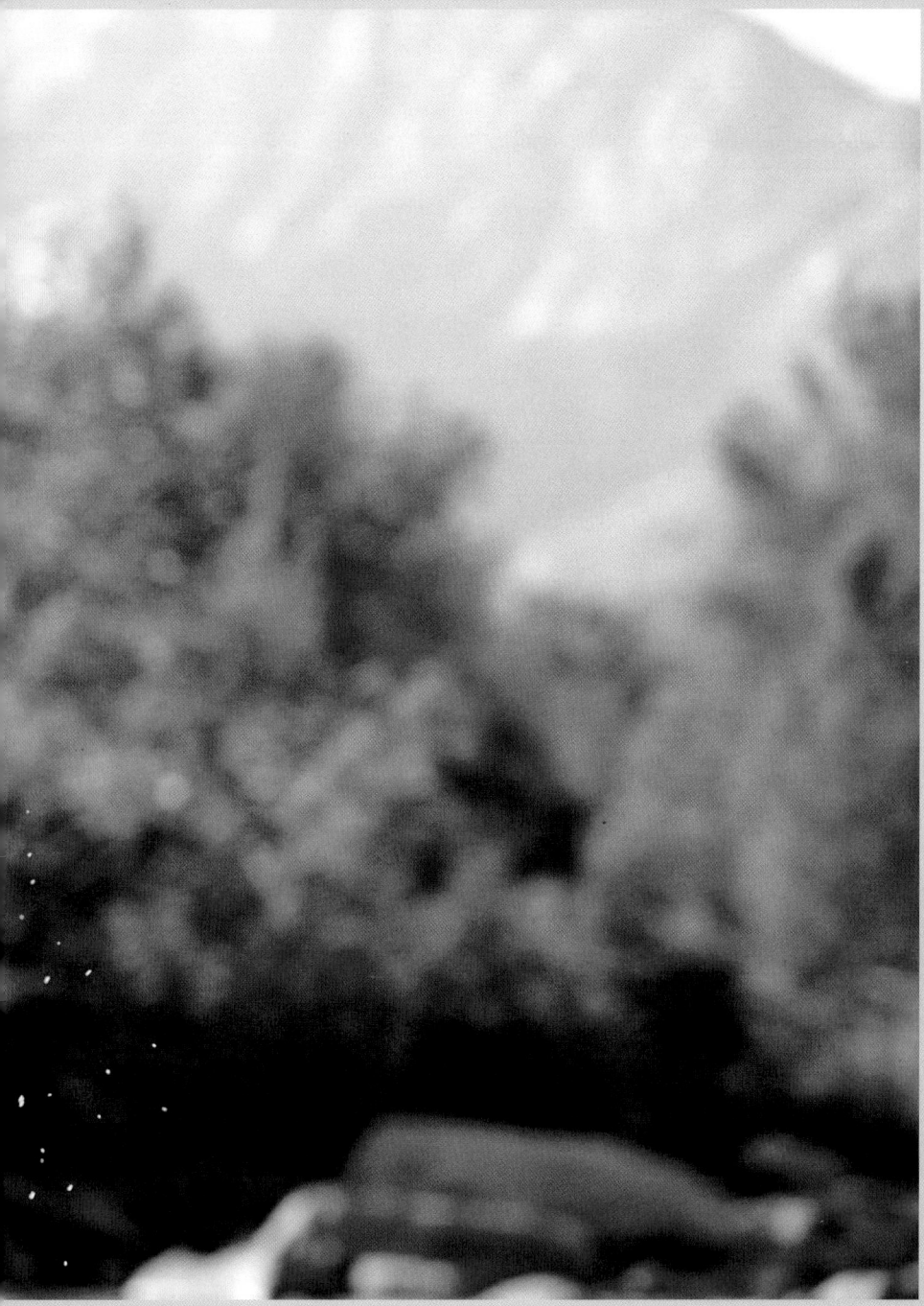

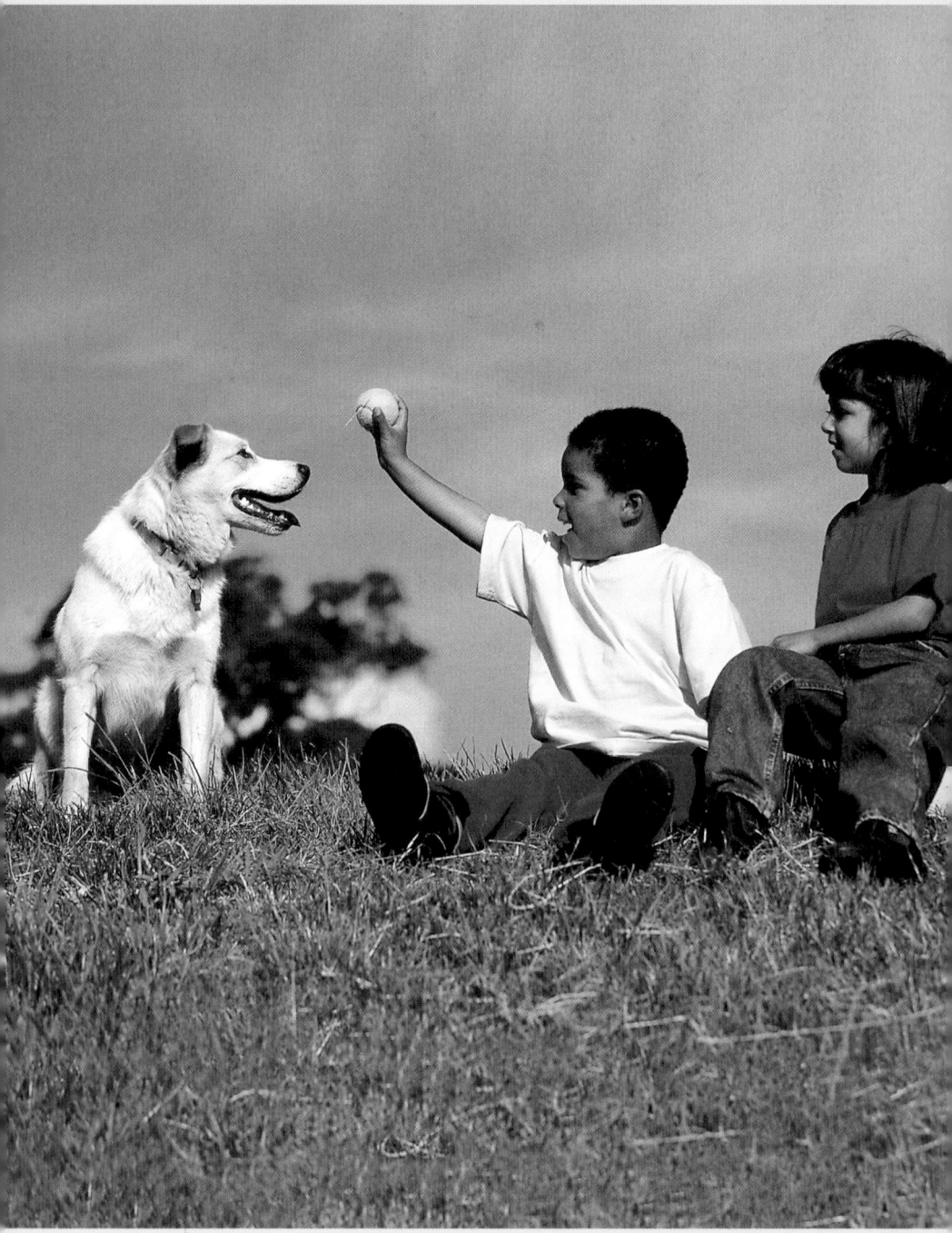